HENRI COLE *Pierce the Skin*

Henri Cole was born in Fukuoka, Japan, and was raised
in Virginia. The recipient of many awards, he is the
author, most recently, of *Blackbird and Wolf* (FSG, 2007)
and *Middle Earth* (FSG, 2003), a Pulitzer Prize finalist.

Blackbird and Wolf

Middle Earth

The Visible Man

The Look of Things

The Zoo Wheel of Knowledge

The Marble Queen

PIERCE THE SKIN

HENRI COLE

Pierce the Skin

SELECTED POEMS

1982–2007

FARRAR STRAUS GIROUX

NEW YORK

FARRAR STRAUS GIROUX

18 West 18th Street, New York 10011

Printed in the United States of America

Published in 2010 by Farrar, Straus and Giroux

First paperback edition, 2011

The Library of Congress has cataloged
the hardcover edition as follows:

Cole, Henri.

Pierce the skin : selected poems / Henri Cole.

p. cm.

ISBN: 978-0-374-23283-2 (hardcover : alk. paper)

I. Title.

PS3553.O45725P54 2011

811'.54—dc22

2009015654

Paperback ISBN: 978-0-374-53266-6

Designed by Quemadura

www.fsgbooks.com

P1

FOR JONATHAN GALASSI

CONTENTS

FROM *The Visible Man* (1998)

FROM *Middle Earth* (2003)

FROM

The Marble Queen

1986

V-winged and Hoary

All our pink and gold and blue
birds have gone to Panama or Peru:

the willow flycatcher with its sneezy "fitzbew,"
the ruby-throated hummingbird with jewel-

like gorgets and the blue-rumped finch,
its song a warble with a guttural "chink."

Far, far across the ghostly frozen lake,
above the great drifts of snow swaying

like dunes, the frosty Iceland gulls,
pallid as beach fleas, make great loops and catfall

into the wind. They are all that is left.
Throngs of children tiptoe deftly

across the lake to watch the robust birds
plunge headlong into kamikaze dives, lured

by fledgling trout nosed against the shallow ice.
Despite the precarious ice,

the children huddle bundled at the edge:
mittened, scarved, and starry-eyed,

their teeth chattering in the frosty air.
They watch the tireless birds, over and over,

fall from the speckled sky, their downy underwings
and pink, taloned leggings

foam soaked as they grapple with their catch.
The children are in love with the miraculous

oval-lipped trout swimming upward for air.
Snowflakes fall against their

cracked lips as they wait, their mouths agape
in little Os at the spectacle of gulls.

Heart of the Monarch

Lesser fritillaries or crescents might
have lost their tribe in the Piedmont,
or some wayward zone, sailing northward like
tiny spinnakers over upper-austral regions

of deciduous hickory and gum,
but near where flat coastal plains
verge westward across forests, overcome
by spring, the African-winged, black-veined

monarchs revive across the temperate
Mayish sky. Assembling each late noon
for sleep, the young bachelor males alight
in unison, the flash and dazzle of venation

klatched near a pond's muddy crevasse.
This puddle club of monarchs, weary and peaceful,
dozes — unappetizing to the thrasher,
the rough-winged swallow, or the needle-

billed hummingbird—abdomens chock-full
of milkweed, foul-tasting to hungry fowl.
So this sleeping assembly, fearless, roosts till
morning, when the herd ascends, their spiracles

yawning as they make their way, steadfast.
Out of vivariums, out of seclusion
from under stones and turfy grass, the half-
grown caterpillar emerges; out of unsewn

mats of silk; out of winter lethargy,
the hibernating chrysalis unruffles
its royal self, its larval life a wee
memory; out of the land of Nod, adults

begin their lazy, deliberate flights
(the conspicuous *monarchs*, mind you, not
the miniature, mimicking *viceroy*!)—
these flower-eating kings, farsighted,

as they make their way with antennae
precision across the psalm of America
toward Milwaukee and Manitoba.
There's nothing to fear. They're on their way.

The Mare

I remember the shade where I found her
spent and bruised like the fallen apples.
Like them, she was full of darkness,
full of the sweetness which rushes upon us
so soon after death.
She lay there like a mummy,
like the wreckage of an ancient queen,
mild, yet locked away within herself.
It held me the long afternoon —
the secret fruit, the silken mare —
until the day had passed.
I stood and walked among the goats
with their delicate steps
and fed them apples
so mellow
they burst like hearts before the queen and me.

The Marble Queen

Beneath the whorish scent of magnolia,
we watch the parade
spill like a river across the avenue before us.

There in the shade I am the child
whistling at the first tide of soldiers,
their boyish hair cropped beneath berets.

There in the shade is Mother,
fixed in her common, girlish pose,
her slim legs tucked beneath her.

She pats the blanket beside her,
dusts a fly from her cheek,
then all at once runs her fingers through her hair

until they catch and snap free into the air.
I watch the blue material of her dress
dimple and lift with each gust of wind.

I am happy, I am sad, dazzled
by the wonderland of uniforms that blurs before us.
Which one is me?

I am the child with his magnifying glass
blazing the hearts from insects,
then scattering the skeletal ash.

In the gentle dreams of this child,
I could match any battalion at war like a giant
and descend from the heavens on my beanstalk

to monitor the sagging world below.
And once I'd grumbled fitfully,
left the armies bewildered like ants

amidst their hills in the ordinary geraniums,
I would ascend my fertile stalk
toward the moonlight of home.

But Mother is thinking of something else—
something beyond the river of men
marching into the pastures of violet

and violet-orange haze where they may fall,
something beyond the young son she has brought
to witness their regaling of strength—

as if the parade has caught her conscience,
and in her conscience, a thousand other women.
Some unforgettable picture wells inside her

until she sees it hovering
like the bees and mayflies humming
in the blue afternoon—

there so long, so simple,
she has misunderstood it:
the terrible monotonous despair.

And now she sits alone with it,
finds expression for it like a child
dreaming of shadows, waiting

for her mother and father to shake her from it.
And when all the armies have passed,
only their footsteps faint in the immense sunlight,

she tamps the half-moons of her eyelashes,
rises before me like a marble queen,
and seizes herself from it.

Father's Jewelry Box

Home for a weekend retreat
   in the tweezered suburbs with Mother
and her four-columned Colonial
   off Colt's Neck cul-de-sac,
she away at the hairdresser
   near the Giant, I make a snoop
at her done-over bedroom,
   Louis Quinze, the blue catalog ensemble,
lovelorn but lovely, and in the feast
   of Father's sleepy chest
of drawers, beneath a rainbow of boxer
   shorts and a pile of bobbed socks,
I find, brassy, fleur-de-lised, and looking-
   glassed, Father's jewelry box.

Caught in a single gasp, the treasure unsnapped,
   the contents a forgotten (forbidden?) potluck:
one copper "BVM," the Mother of Jesus
   faint behind a veil of oxidation,
cozily fastened to Daddy's war-proof
   dog tags worn like a patriarchal

cross across five continents;
   five baby teeth—two cavitied,
two female and three male—plucked
   from each of us tots;
one crystal earring flashing like a javelin;
   monogrammed studs and links for penguin
attire; a Masonic medallion with an eye-
   of-God as sad as a crocodile's;

the vague odor of cologne, of hairbrush,
   of body scent from ribbons starred
and striped; an awful Purple Heart;
   a gold wedding band inscribed in Roman caps:
UNTIL THE LAST—yet never worn as Father
   probed the galvanic gut of machinery,
the ring a volcanic conductor of electricity
   inducing cardiac arrest.
All this to the tune of "Stardust,"
   its melody lulling as Mother arrives
coiffed from the Giant, her bosom breathless
   as she catches me by surprise: "Good heavens!"—
but I am neither, pirating an oyster's pearl from her room,
   my head fogged with the scent of her perfume.

FROM

The Zoo Wheel
of Knowledge

1989

The Annulment

FOR MY NEPHEW

After a time, because they could not love
one another as they could others,
what became of you recalled my infant brother,
lost in Limbo, his breath elusive
as crib death, waiting in a field for the world's end.
So when the church unleashed them from their hearts,
undoing the words that were forever, through the dark
glass there was nothing but her earrings golden
in the moonlight and the torque of his neck as he
raced the motor of their Triumph. Though they
transgressed and wandered incalculably,
you rose out of them, lacquered from your journey
and muttering vowels like all the lost children,
souls breathed forth, sitting up in their graves to sing.

A Half-life

There is no sun today,
except the finch's yellow breast,
and the world seems faultless in spite of it.
Across the sound, a continuous
ectoplasm of gray,
a ferry slits deep waters,

bumping the tiny motorboats
against their pier.
The day ends like any day,
with its hour of human change
lifting the choleric heart.
If living in someone else's dream

makes us soft, then I am so,
spilling out from the lungs
like the green phlegm of spring.
My friend resting on the daybed
fills his heart with memory,
while July's faithful swallows

weave figure eights above him,
vaulting with pointed wings and forked tails

for the ripe cherries he tosses them,
then ascending in a frolic
of fanned umbrella-feathers
to thread a far, airy steeple.

To my mind, the cherries from an endless
necklacelike cortex rising out
of my friend's brain, the swallows
unraveling the cerebellum's pink cord.
In remission six months, his
body novocained and fallow,

he trembles, threadbare, as the birds unwheel him.
The early evening's furnace casts
us both in a shimmering sweat.
In a wisp Gabriel might appear to us,
as if to Mary, announcing a sweet
miracle. But there is none.

The lilies pack in their trumpets,
our nesting dove nuzzles her eggs,
and chameleons color their skin with dusk.
A half-life can be deepened by a whole,
sending out signals of a sixth sense,
as if the unabashed, youthful eye

sees clearest to the other side.
A lemon slice spirals in the icy tea,

a final crystal pulse of sun reappears,
and a newer infinite sight
takes hold of us, like the jet of color
at the end of winter. Has it begun:

the strange electric vision of the dying?
Give me your hand, friend.
Come see the travelers arrive.
Beneath the lazy, bankrupt sky,
theirs is a world of joy trancing
even the gulls above the silver ferry.

White Sheets

Our car sped down into the earth,
rollers and cables snaking past us,
my hand pressing in on my sister's,
until we landed against a buffer
and the chrome gates slid open.

The rooms were scrubbed and neat
with a yellowish glow, the men tense
with their enterprise. When he saw us,
he doffed his cap and picked me up,
twizzling his breath in my ear.
A life intransigently beautiful,
of Father's books, of Mother's china,
was left, I knew, inexplicably behind.
It was the furthest I could see
through childhood's eyes: all that we are
or could be was beating blood and salt.

The men listened in their headsets
for tremors from a country armored

as a battalion of steel, for hydrogen
eggs, big as a dinosaur's, testing
beneath the earth's shield,
the flames and asbestos-suits unrevealed.
I bounced my tennis ball against a wall,
while across a gunmetal ocean
Khrushchev zoned the world under sickle and star.
Time, our infant sibling, was stumbling
with us through history,
surging like the white sheets
that draped the headquarters' walls,
hung for our visit, concealing
seismographic charts and bright blowups
of quartered hemispheres.

                If all of them
had loved — it burned in me — like John Rolfe
and Pocahontas wedded in my textbook
(not to speak of Reverend King,
who'd yet to fall that awful spring),
unafraid of defeat, mightn't the terror
have flattened as under a tank's treads,
or as in art, where inexhaustible darkness
can be cast out by tenderness?

                The rage,
even its complete mastery, is not enough.

This morning, long afterward, in the gray
confusion of spring, rain streaming in the trees,
that vanished hour came back to me,
and how beyond all this, as I was
dandled upon a knee, my ears
popped from the subterranean air.

Ascension on Fire Island

No octopus-candelabra
    or baby Jesus adorns
the summerhouse we gather in
    to sing a hymn of forgiveness.
No church bells bronzed overhead
    ring and set our eager mob free
when the service is said.
    Only curtains in a strong wind,

billowing like spinnakers
    upon us, seem a godly sign,
or almost so. Sharp as a new pin,
    the day begins around us,
a speckled doe nibbling
    petunias as we pray,
an excess of elementals
    piloting us forward, like Polaris,

into the Gospel's verbal cathedral.
    As when Jesus appeared
to the eleven while they sat at meat

and upbraided them for their
unbelief and hardness of heart,
  our congregation seems unknowing
at first of goodness yet to come.
   Is there a god unvexed to protect us?

What pious group wouldn't have it so!
The floor creaks beneath us
like the hull of a ship,
  and the surf purrs in the distance,
confounding us with place,
   until a cardinal alights, twig-flexing,
anchoring us with his featherweight.
   Listen for the passing stillness . . .

In the harbor a man floats
  portside of his sloop, his purple
Windbreaker flashing in a sunburst.
  Let him be forgiven, this once,
who put him there. The family squabble,
   the bruised cranium, piece by piece,
will face up to light of day.
  And the body, its brief

unimmaculate youth, will be hoisted
  from the water's patina of calm.

The nervous deer, the cardinal,
    our perfect citizen, even invisible
bells aloft press in upon us
    with sheltering mystery,
as in the distance a throng gathers
    and the yellow death-blanket unfolds.

The Zoo Wheel of Knowledge

FOR CHRISTOPHER BRAM AND DRAPER SHREEVE

The difficulty to see at the end of the day:
she's sprinkling flour in the bronze light,
he's spooning apricots into our infant,
and Star, marauder of the yards and alleys,

is sleeping in the next room, wiggling
on his haunches, ears flapping, his red eyes
in a dream rushing away with their catch,
his tongue a spear in our hearts.

How strange to hear in the fading sun
the little girls from Sacred Heart scream
and rush against each other when the lions
in the park let go their convulsive roar,

awakening in us, as with the addict,
a spasmlike hunger to please the beast.
So we set off, all of us, guiding out stroller,
the baby's head floating before us through

the dark, arctic tanks where the bears
glide, monsterlike yet sultry,
their eyes opening, brown as Mother's,
at the viewing window, their phosphorescent

trunks so white and godlike
a neighbor's sons, one night, scaled the wall
to dive and kick among them.
Pity the poor beasts, weary, gazing upward—

except the congress of bats asleep in its cave—
as if at the stars that mirror them
in constellation: Pavo, the peacock;
tough-skinned Leo; the gold-fleeced ram;

Aquila, the eagle; even little Lepus, the hare,
whom all the children pet at the petting station.
Whatever happens to them, mishap or fortune,
is as well for us with downy fur on our spines.

Each child freezes them in Kodak—
above us the ape's lips are cracked and bleeding,
his pink tits pumped up from swinging
in the canopy—and therefore ourselves

in rendezvous this first light of evening,
as if at a pageant or crazy fantasia
of the unconscious where we all collect
eventually, even Star and the souls

of the boys found in the polar tank,
all of us writhing in a kind of heroic
remembering of what our natures are —
the unspeakable resemblance, the distant

mother tongue — though the cage bars
frame us apart. The gold eyes
look outward, nearly bodiless in the dim light,
as if in that halcyon moment when bison, herding,

lift their flecked heads all at once toward
the hills, knowing they'll take possession.
Oh, Lord, make us sure as the beasts
who drink from the pond, their shaggy manes

dappled with air; who see those that flee
from them, yet wait and breathe accustomed
to the night; and who listen tirelessly
for grasses to blow on the plain again.

FROM

The Look of Things

1995

The Pink and the Black

The sea a goblet of black currant liqueur.
The pink sky regarding me sadly.
The hand that was mine, motionless,
   between passages in a story.
The sucking sound of underwater breathing, spitting.
The limy bubbles sequinning the sea.
The mutable shape we call man, rising out of it,
   all nostrils and lips behind glass.
The Day-Glo flippers striking against limestone,
   like a Spanish fan on pearls.
The limp, saclike bodies, pink suckers in perfect rows,
   hooked at the belt.
The oyster-white rock on which we sat.
The sleepy face that looked at me.
The crossed ankles.
The inky cloud, like an octopus's secretion,
   moving overhead.
The sun a watery white mess.
The dainty, crocheted net where the sea urchins slept.
The long spines of the one shucked for me.
The bowie knife, sharp as a curate's words, cutting, cutting.

The intractable sea flattening and flattening.
The metallic back of something escaping,
  reveling beneath the shadows.
I had been so lonely, hungry as a snake.

Paper Dolls

To some it might
have seemed vulgar
or degrading that
he was naked
but for a wrinkled sheet.
Straight as candles,
his legs exposed
the eroding candelabrum
that was his body.
As directed,
no priest was present,
so when his mouth,
chapped and bleeding,
locked on a breath
we believed was the last,
the other of us
ran wailing down
the long blue corridor
for a nurse,
who came to us
as Demeter had
to the frozen earth.

On the windowsill,
red tulips
stopped their grieving
as we kissed
what remained
goodbye
in a scene
at first holy,
then lurid,
as something stirred
beneath the sheet.
On the night table,
paper dolls cut
like shackled lions
roared at his entrance.

40 Days and 40 Nights

Opening a vein he called my radial,
the phlebotomist introduced himself as Angel.
Since the counseling it had been ten days
of deep inversion — self-recrimination weighed
against regret, those useless emotions.
Now there would be thirty more enduring the notion
of some self-made doom foretold in the palm.

Waiting for blood work with aristocratic calm,
big expectant mothers from Spanish Harlem
appeared cut out, as if Matisse had conceived them.
Their bright smocks ruffling like plumage before the fan,
they might themselves have been angels come by land.

Consent and disclosure signed away, liquid gold
of urine glimmering in a plastic cup, threshold
of last doubt crossed, the red fluid was drawn
in a steady hematic ooze from my arm.
"Now, darling, the body doesn't lie," Angel said.
DNA and enzymes and antigens in his head
true as lines in the face in the mirror
on his desk.

I smiled, pretending to be cheered.
In the way that some become aware of God
when they cease becoming overawed
with themselves, no less than the artist concealed
behind the surface of whatever object or felt
words he builds, so I in my first week
of waiting let the self be displaced by each
day's simplest events, letting them speak
with emblematic voices that might teach me.
They did . . . until I happened on the card
from the clinic, black framed as a graveyard.
Could the code 12 22 90 have represented
some near time, December 22, 1990, for repentance?
The second week I believed it. The fourth I
rejected it and much else loved, until the eyes
teared those last days and the lab phoned.

Back at the clinic — someone's cheap cologne,
Sunday lamb yet on the tongue, the mind cool as a pitcher
of milk, a woman's knitting needles aflutter,
Angel's hand in mine — I watched the verdict-lips move,
rubbed my arm, which, once pricked, had tingled, then bruised.

The Roman Baths at Nîmes

In the hall of mirrors, nobody speaks.
An ember smolders before hollowed cheeks.
Someone empties pockets, loose change and keys,
into a locker. My God forgives me.
Some say love, disclosed, repels what it sees,
yet if I touch the darkness, it touches me.
In the steam room, inconsolable tears
fall against us. In the whirlpool, my arms,
rowing through little green crests, help to steer
the body, riding against death. Yet what harm
is there in us? I swear to you, my friend,
cross-armed in a bright beach towel, turning round
to see my face in the lamplight, that eye, ear,
and tongue, good things, make something sweet of fear.

You Come When I Call You

I was very trusting and very dangerous
the night Committee Members arrived.
Something that smelled like wet dog wrapped my eyes.
Sleeping naked, I was permitted to dress,
as someone explained how by white- and black-
ball election I was last among their choices.
At first, the friendly timbre of the voices
comforted me . . . until I was prodded like an ass
into a truck (or like the missing child Jed,
I remember thinking, whose face appeared
on my milk carton), where I could hear
others, like me, breathing prostrate on the flatbed
and the zealous talk of Brotherhood
at their seats in the cab. Drinking from flasks,
they jeered at us in our doggy masks.
Though we could not see, how we understood!

They steered us to a lake in the Commonwealth,
and, speaking in a language designated
by little Greek letters, revealed themselves
as a court for the uninitiated.
A man must make do the best he can

in a world where goodness is stamped out:
this much I resolved that humid morning South,
as I drank, kneeling like a broken man,
from a sulfur spring with other Pledges,
then pressed my lips in adoration to pages
of a book held before me. "A French kiss!
She's giving it the tongue!" the Chairman hissed.
Then suddenly the proceedings ended.

My wrists and red eyes untied, I was asked
to sing songs the Little Sisters, steadfast
behind their Brothers, belted out. Legends
of Reconstruction teach us a few good things.
About pride, for instance, and how a ruined
land with hospitals and barracks was soon
our little college. Yet in that lamentable
fraternal Gamma code I found not one
natural Brother, only niggling dues to be paid,
committees, like dogs paraded
on leashes, straining toward women,
immolation of spirit, a berated
God, nobility worn like a harness,
a sour apple in the heart, and this,
this was the congenial state I'd awaited.

The Minimum Circus

FOR MARY DOYLE SPRINGER

From the marks on their coats
and the unambiguous wag
    of their tails as they sniff
each other, one can see they are
    related—all the dogs
in our neighborhood circling a quay
    in the port, awaiting
the circus pushcart carrying
    four dazed French house cats, who,
unperplexed, crawl through tubes, jump hoops,
    balance on a high wire,
and ride an irritable goat bareback.

The sweet ringmaster, who
has no teeth, wears Cézanne's straw hat
    and borrowed evening tails.
It has taken him years to stage
    the flawless *tigres* act.
He has a distant, sympathetic heart.

When Madame Pompinette,
a pretty white thing, is let out
of her little wood box,
she does ballerina stretches,
carefully licking each
murderous claw, making the dogs go wild.

Backed up on their haunches,
with pointed ears, they do not hear
moody Debussy as
Madame crosses a perilous
clothesline to her platform
and relaxes. Welcome as tears boldly
shed, the cats transcend class.
Coming no less from Arab shacks
on vineyards than from big
summer châteaux, the hounds escape
their odious lot,
drinking and drinking in the cats, who eat

sardines and seem to laugh.
When the ringmaster's hat is passed,
he cracks his lion-whip
like Mallarmé yearning for some
daring, inward effect.
My ten-franc piece hardly speaks to the cats,

who repose with laissez-faire
expressions, like humans given
a mask, willing to tell
the truth of their predicament,
as if to say to me:
"This is what life is supposed to be."

Harvard Classics

It is the hour of lamps.
On our knees my mother
and I, still young, color
with crayons threadbare nap

on the living room rug.
Though there is no money,
no one seems to care. We
are self-possessed as bugs

waving their antennae
through cracks in the kitchen's
linoleum floor. When
Father begins to read

from the red gilt volume
in his lap, a circle
of light encapsulates
us like hearts in a womb.

Except their marriage is
already dead. I know

this though I'm only six.
So we visit pharaohs,

a boatman on the Nile,
Crusaders eating grapes
on a beach. Life escapes
with all its sadness while

two tragic Greek poets
inhabit Father's voice.
Who'd know I am just a boy
when he begins a stoic

moral tale concerning
a dull provincial doctor's
young French wife? If Mother,
in French, begins to sing

to herself, I know she's
had enough. Crayon stubs
litter the crumbling rug.
Our prostrate cat sneezes

at the dust in her fur.
And cries from a swallow
remind us one swallow
doesn't make a summer.

Une Lettre à New York

If it's spring in the city, have the marchers,
each one with a shrieking whistle, short-circuited the streets,
their cause as grave as the dirty cabs growling at their feet?
Is Paul Taylor at City Center? Has my architecture-
grad-student subtenant remembered Sting, a pet squirrel
whose appearance each May on the fire escape ledge
is a celebrated as our pink dogwood's flowering? Privileged
as she is, eating Arabian almonds all these years, if she's early
and hears me in the shower, she knows to come right in.
Will Joe, my Italian barber, still tell me what to do in life,
reading my moods in his mirror—his razor like a fruit knife
against the peach's flesh instead of the proud artist's chin?
Will a burglar have borrowed my red Schwinn from the rooftop,
the rusty chain foiling his smooth delirious escape?
With pom-poms swinging on their skimmers like grapes,
does a Colombian troupe still serenade commuters stopped,
even in gray business suits, by a tug on the heartstrings,
the subway chasm converted into a dream of disembarking?
Does the beggar on my block, who says his name is Marx,
still wear a deeper tan than mine? Will souls of three sleeping
friends—May, Lola, and Vladimir—visit in the evening,
arranging themselves in the ailanthus outside my window?

If they smile and blink as from some Broadway video,
it will be an urban bequest for those who could not say goodbye,
their numinous bodies dissolving then into July's fireflies,
whose lanterns alchemize my cheap paper shades into Chinese silk.
Each of you who writes reports illness, pain from love spilt,
or someone who's gone to the other side, yet correspondence tries
to be uplifting, disapproving Judas, who writes man's sad history.
Could he have been right who said there was earth and man
in the beginning, that we created God, that we created heaven
in our want or need for something more than awful elegy?
The little island wedged between three rivers,
from which our letters come and go, is the personification of hope.
The buildings are black and white like sonnets. And enveloped
in between the first sweet cherries of the season are being delivered.

Tarantula

At a pet shop in the village,
in a battered gothic cage,
he stood guard (or was kept hostage?)

at a little parapet trap-
door. His dirty home was so sad,
his burrow a curled-up scrap

of carpet, that I unscrewed
the wire gate with my Swiss knife — DO
NOT UNSCREW!, it read — and let him through.

Ten stiff bristles uplifted him,
each a comb for his hairy abdomen,
his front legs now and again

waving in an attitude of bliss
as he swayed upon my wrist.
Then gliding like a dugout canoe, its

oars moving in a phalanx,
he rowed across my long arm, strangely
beautiful as the human brain

shining through profligate grief.
When he looked at me with a queer
air, nearsighted as I, did he make me

out to be a giant fern, his perch,
as I have made him now into a verse?
When his creaky spinneret stirred,

I felt guilt—watching him create
a silky floating line in haste—
knowing a sad house has no escape.

Buddha and the Seven Tiger Cubs

Holding a varnished paper parasol,
the gardener—a shy man off the street—
rakes the white sand, despite rainfall,
into a pattern effortlessly neat,
meant to suggest, only abstractly, the sea,
as eight weathered stones are meant to depict
Buddha and the hungry cubs he knows he
must sacrifice himself to feed. I sit
in a little red gazebo and think—
as the Zen monks do—about what love means,
unashamed to have known it as something
tawdry and elusive from watching lean
erotic dancers in one of the dives
on Stark Street, where I go on lovesick nights.

Even in costume they look underage,
despite hard physiques and frozen glances
perfected for the ugly, floodlit stage,
where they're stranded like fish. What enhances
their act is that we're an obedient crowd,
rheumy with liquor; our stinginess
is broken. When one slings his leg proudly

across the bar rail where I sit, I kiss
a five-dollar bill and tuck it in his belt.
He's a black swan straining its elastic
neck to eat bread crumbs and nourish itself.
My heart is not alert; I am transfixed,
loving him as tiger cubs love the mother
who abandons them forever.

Apostasy

Father, when, when, when will you lift me,
dirty baby, from my crib?
With pail and shovel, I dig, dig for you,
scratching the earth like a hen.
When I pull her cord, my mermaid doll,
with flaxen hair, says strange things:
"Sooner dead than changed!"
Could she be speaking of you, Father?
Well, if that's what Mermaid believes,
Mermaid cannot come to tea.
Or the others, Father, piled like puppies
at my feet: nursing shark, green toad
with red tongue, rubber goldfish —
who come to parties I set for them
with Mother's blue Fiesta ware,
singing Hawaiian songs, eating shortbread.
"Dirty Baby, Dirty Baby," you say to me,
when I nuzzle my wet face against your neck.
Dirty Baby loves the taste of flesh.
Dirty Baby needs you to cut his meat.
Dirty Baby needs you to teach him how to chew.

The Visible Man

1998

White Spine

Liar, I thought, kneeling with the others,
how can He love me and hate what I am?
The dome of St. Peter's shone yellowish
gold, like butter and eggs. My God, I prayed
anyhow, as if made in the image
and likeness of Him. Nearby, a handsome
priest looked at me like a stone; I looked back,
not desiring to go it alone.
The college of cardinals wore punitive red.
The white spine waved to me from his white throne.
Being in a place not my own, much less
myself, I climbed out, a beast in a crib.
Somewhere a terrorist rolled a cigarette.
Reason, not faith, would change him.

Adam Dying

(PIERO DELLA FRANCESCA, THE STORY

OF ADAM. AREZZO, SAN FRANCESCO)

Though the most we can say is that it is
as if there were a world before Adam,
even that seems narrow and parochial
as we contemplate his dying ... while Eve,
with withered breasts, watches pensively,
and the mellifluous young, in animal skins,
stand about emotionless, like pottery.
What do the significant glances mean?

Can only Adam—naked, decrepit,
sprawled in the dirt—see what dying is?
How can they not hear the moaning, smell the body,
suffer the burden of original sin?
East & West, armies revile each other.
Mothers hunt among the decomposing dead.

FROM *Chiffon Morning*

I

I am lying in bed with my mother,
where my father seldom lay. Little poem,
help me to say all I need to say, better.
Hair dyed, combed; nails polished; necklacelike scar
ear-to-ear; stocky peasant's bulk hidden
under an unfeminine nightgown; sour-milk
breaths rehearsing death, she faces me, her room
a pill museum where orange tea bags
draining on napkins almost pass for art.
Even the Christmas amaryllis sags
under the weight of its bloodred
petals, unfolding like a handkerchief.
From the television screen, a beauty
pageant queen waves serenely at me.

II

In the oily black barbecue smoke,
in our blue Chevrolet station wagon,
in a cottage at the sea, no one spoke

but me to the nerveless God
who never once stopped their loveless act:
the cursing mouths, the shoving and choking,
the violent pulse, the wrecked hair, the hunchbacked
reprisal, the suddenly inverted sky,
the fiendish gasping, the blade that cuts all
understanding, the white knuckles, the fly
remarkably poised on a blue throat.
I try to pity them. Perhaps God did
on those occasions when battle was a prelude
to sex, and peace, like an arrow, found us.

V

As the cuckoo clock crows in the kitchen,
on her nightstand others as bluntly chime
but cannot break her drugged oblivion.
Please wake up, Mother, and wet your cottonmouth.
"She was agitated," nurses whispered
when we found her tied to the bed, knocked out.
Demerol blocked the pain, entering through the eyes,
while the mind, crushed like a wineglass, healed.
"I'll bury you all," she gloated, at home again.
Months later, they stitched her throat in surgery.
The voice that had been on the radio

when the war was on plunged a tragic octave.
More pills crowded her daily glass of milk.
My guilt seemed vain compared to what she felt.

VI

Mother is naked and holding me up
above her as soap streams from my face
(I'm wearing a dumb ape's frown) into the tub
where she is seated: the mind replays
what nurtures it. The black months when she
would lie assassinated like our Siamese cat
are still far off. Yet, tranced by a lush light,
which no one else sees, like a leaden bee
shackled to a poppy, I am not free.
Each time I am dunked in the green, green
sacramental water, I glare shamelessly
as she shrieks and kisses me, gripped in air;
I do not know if she loves me or cares,
if it's suffering or joy behind her tears.

The Coast Guard Station

At dawn, a few recruits have a smoke
on the patio above the breakers;
across the sand path, I sit with my books,
hearing their animal coughs.

Strangely, watching them tranquilizes me.
Their big clapboard house
is illuminated all night,
like the unconscious, though no one enters.
Even in hallucinatory fog,
their pier is flashbulb bright
and staunch as Abraham.
Overhead, a gull scavenges like a bare hand.
An officer, in orange overalls,
stares like a python
up into the window where I am.

What does it mean to be chosen?
To have your body grow into a hero's
and have done nothing to achieve it?
To seize a birthright, unobstructed?
To dominate with confident bearing?

That is their covenant,
even cold-stupefied and lethargic:
hearing the blessing of Isaac to Jacob.
Naked and a little drunk,
I sit chafing at it,
the nerves in my teeth aching,
lording it over the rest of me.

Why do I appear to be what I am not?
To the world, arrogantly self-sufficient.
To myself, womanish, conflicted, subservient,
like Esau pleading, "Bless me also, Father!"
I hate what I am and I hate what I am not.

Horses

Setting out on my bicycle alone,
I came upon the horses
drenched in bright sunshine,
yard after yard of blue-black ironed silk,
drawn before stopped traffic.

With white stars on their foreheads
and white bracelets on their legs,
each blood horse wore nothing
but a fine noseband
and a shroud of steam.

I felt lazy and vicious watching them,
with my large joints and big head,
stricken by thoughts of my brothers.
If only the barbarous horsemen
could lead *us* down the path, unestranged.

It smashed in me like water galloped through.
Flinching there on my haunches,
with wide nostrils,
nipping the air as if it were green grass,
how I yearned for my neck to be brushed!

Black Mane

Do you hear him, how he's asking?
Say something to him.
Let him feel your presence.

When he paws the ground, lies down, and rolls luxuriously,
when he stands up, shakes the dust off, and snorts vigorously,
do not stand in his shadow.
Go to him. Grasp his mane,
like the handle of a coffin, and climb on.
Don't worry, he will be patient with you.
He sees you laid bare riding him,
following his head like a lovesick pupil.
He knows you will not raise your crop to him.
He feels your flesh twitching against his.

At last you have what you longed for,
as if man on a horse constituted a single creature,
like a man on a high rock
at the edge of a field.
But now the creature leaps about the field,
the self is not a lonely figure in the sun.
The days when you lay his reins in a loop on his withers
and stand beside him, groping his neck,

if he lays back his ears and bares his teeth,
do not feel unworthy.
Body & soul cannot always
be alive together.

Walk, trot, stop, turn—these are only words
and yet he obeys them, obedient and calm.
His surrender is not a servile thing.
His power is born not of muscle and blood,
but of a self, like a monument
excavated in the sun.
Feel how your soul burns hard
and is changed by him?
See how he fears and respects you
without fact or reason?
See him looking straight ahead
as if it were Hadrian on his back?
Rub molasses on his bit
and he'll fling his heels in a capriole.

When your body sorrows into his,
it is as if a bolt were pushed into place,
metal hitting metal, like wisdom.
And his body, bridled and saddled, conveying yours,
brings nothing like grace or redemption,
those taming biblical things,
but like a wave, like a loud chord, like a masterpiece

of oiled canvas, it brings a pulsing, an incessant ravening,
like a robin pouncing at a worm, that nurses
the individuated being, like a tight bud,
into something unsparing while blooming,
and electric, like a paddock fence,
making all that is contained within it
aware of all that is not,
as ash in an urn
must remember the flesh it once was.

FROM *Apollo*

I

With a shriek gulls fled across a black sky,
all of us under the pier were silent,
my blood ached from waiting, then we resumed.
"You're just like us," some bastard said;
and it was true: my hair was close cropped,
my frame reposed against a piling, my teeth
glistened, my prick was stiff. Little by little
they had made me like them, raptly feeding
in silhouette, with exposed abdomen,
like a spider sating itself. For a moment,
I was the eye through which the universe
beheld itself, like God. And then I gagged,
stumbling through brute shadows to take a piss,
a fly investigating my wet face.

11

Stay married, God said. One marriage.

　　　　Don't abortion. Ugly mortal sin.
Beautiful gorgeous Mary loves you
　　　　so much. Heaven tremendous thrill
of ecstasy forever. What you are,
　　　　they once was, God said, the beloved ones
before you; what they are, you will be.
　　　　All the days. Don't fornicate. Pray be good.
Serpent belly thorn and dust. Serpent belly
　　　　sing lullaby. Beautiful gorgeous Jesus
love you so much. Only way to heaven
　　　　church on Sunday. You must pray rosary.
Toil in fields. Heaven tremendous thrill
　　　　of ecstasy forever. Don't fornicate.

IV

The search for a single dominant gene—
"the 'O-God' hypothesis" (one-gene,
one disorder)—which, like an oracle,
foreknows the sexual brain, is fruitless.

The human self is undeconstructable
montage, is poverty, learning, & war,
is DNA, words, is acts in a bucket,
is agony and love on a wheel that sparkles,

is a mother and father creating
and destroying, is mutable
and one with God, is man and wife speaking,
is innocence betrayed by justice,

is not sentimental but sentimentalized,
is a body contained by something bodiless.

VI

On the sand there were dead things from the deep.
Faint-lipped shells appeared and disappeared,
like language assembling out of gray.

Then a seal muscled through the surf,
like a fetus, and squatted on a sewage pipe.
I knelt in the tall grass and grinned at it.

Body and self were one, vaguely
coaxed onward by the monotonous waves,
recording like compound sentences.

The seal was on its way somewhere cold, far.
Nothing about it exceeded what it was
(unlike a soul reversing itself to be

something more or a pen scratching words
on vellum after inking out what came before).

X

To write what is human, not escapist:
that is the problem of the hand moving
apart from my body.
                    Yet, subject is
only pretext for assembling the words
whose real story is process is flow.
So the hand lurches forward, gliding back
serenely, radiant with tears, a million
beings and objects hypnotizing me
as I sit and stare.
                    Not stupefied. Not aching.
Today I am one. The hand jauntily
at home with evil, with unexamined feelings,
with just the facts.
                    Mind and body, like spikes,
like love and hate, recede pleasantly.
Do not be anxious. The hand remembers them.

XI

When I was a boy, our father cooked
to seek forgiveness for making our house
a theater of hysteria and despair.
How could I not eat gluttonously?

You, my Apollo, cannot see that your hands
moving over me, the plainer one,
make me doubt you, that a son's life is punishment
for a father's. Young and penniless,

you serve me lobster. Scalding in the pot,
how it shrieked as I would with nothing left!
Please forgive my little dramas of the self.
And you do . . . in an interruption of the night,

when one body falls against another —
in the endless dragging of chains that signifies love.

XIII CYPARISSUS

"I am here. I will always succor you,"
he used to say, a little full of himself.
What did I know? I was just a boy
loved by Apollo. There had been others.
All I wanted was to ride my deer,
who made me feel some knowledge of myself,
letting me string his big antlers with violets.

One day, in a covert, not seeing the deer
stray to drink at a cool spring, I thrust
my spear inadvertently into him.
Not even Apollo could stop the grief,
which gave me a greenish tint, twisting my
forehead upward; I became a cypress.
Poor Apollo: nothing he loves can live.

XIV

This is not a poem of resurrection.
The body secretes its juices and then is gone.
This is a poem of insurrection
against the self. In the beginning was the child,
fixating on the mother, taking himself
as the sexual object . . . You know the story.
In the mirror I see a man with a firm
masculine body. Mouth open like a fish,
I look at him, one of the lucky ones
above the surface where the real me
is bronzed in the Apollonian sun.
I stay awhile, mesmerized by the glass
whose four corners frame the eyes of a man
I might have been, not liquid, not pent in.

Middle Earth

2003

Self-portrait in a Gold Kimono

Born, I was born.

          Tears represent how much my mother loves me,
shivering and steaming like a horse in rain.

             My heart as innocent as Buddha's,
my name a Parisian bandleader's,

                 I am trying to stand.
Father is holding me and blowing in my ear,

                   like a glassblower on a flame.
Stars on his blue serge uniform flaunt a feeling

              of formal precision and stoicism.
Growing, I am growing now,

          as straight as red pines in the low mountains.
Please don't leave, Grandmother Pearl.

                 I become distressed
watching the president's caisson.

            We, we together move to the big house.
Shining, the sun is shining on my time line.

                Tears, copper-hot tears,
spatter the house

          when Father is drunk, irate, and boisterous.
The essence of self emerges

           shuttling between parents.

Noel, the wet nimbus of Noel's tongue

       draws me out of the pit.

I drop acid with Rita.

     Chez Woo eros is released.

I eat sugar like a canary from a grown man's tongue.

        The draft card torn up;

the war lost.

    I cling like a cicada to the latticework of memory.

Mother: "I have memories, too.

       Don't let me forget them."

Father: "I'm glad the journey is set.

      I'm glad I'm going."

Crows, the voices of crows

     leaving their nests at dawn, circle around,

as I sit in a gold kimono,

     feeling the subterranean magma flows,

the sultry air, the hand holding a pen,

      bending to write,

Thank you,

   Mother and Father, for creating me.

Icarus Breathing

Indestructible seabirds, black and white, leading and following;

semivisible mist, undulating, worming about the head;

rain starring the sea, tearing all over me;

our little boat, as in a Hokusai print, nudging closer

to Icarus (a humpback whale, not a foolish dead boy)

heaving against rough water; a voluminous inward grinding—

like a self breathing, but not a self—revivifying,

oxygenating the blood, making the blowhole move,

like a mouth silent against the decrees of fate: joy, grief,

desperation, triumph. Only God can obstruct them.

A big wave makes my feet slither. I feel like a baby,

bodiless and strange: a man is nothing if he is not changing.

Father, is that you breathing? Forgiveness is anathema to me.

I apologize. Knock me to the floor. Take me with you.

The Hare

The hare does not belong to the rodents;

he is a species apart. Holding him firmly

against my chest, kissing his long white ears,

tasting earth on his fur and breath,

I am plunged into that white sustenance again,

where a long, fathomless calm emerges—

like a love that is futureless but binding

for a body on a gurney submerged in bright light,

as an orchard is submerged in lava—

while the hand of my brother, my companion

in nothingness, strokes our father,

but no power in the air touches us,

as one touches those one loves, as I

stroke a hare trembling in a box of straw.

Kayaks

Beyond the soggy garden, two kayaks

float across mild clear water. A red sun

stains the lake like colored glass. Day is stopping.

Everything I am feels distant or blank

as the opulent rays pass through me,

distant as action is from thought,

or language is from all things desirable

in the world, when it does not deliver

what it promises and pathos comes instead—

the same pathos I feel when I tell myself,

within or without valid structures of love:

I have been deceived, he is not what he seemed—

though the failure is not in the other,

but in me because I am tired, hurt, or bitter.

Radiant Ivory

After the death of my father, I locked

myself in my room, bored and animal-like.

The travel clock, the Johnnie Walker bottle,

the parrot tulips—everything possessed his face,

chaste and obscure. Snow and rain battered the air

white, insane, slathery. Nothing poured

out of me except sensibility, dilated.

It was as if I were *sub*-born—preverbal,

truculent, pure—with hard ivory arms

reaching out into a dark and crowded space,

illuminated like a perforated silver box

or a little room in which glowing cigarettes

came and went, like souls losing magnitude,

but none with the battered hand I knew.

Ape House, Berlin Zoo

Are the lost like this,
living not like a plant, an inch to drink each week,
but like the grass snake under it,
gorging itself before a famine?
Gazing at me longer than any human has in a long time,
you are my closest relative in thousands of miles.
When your soul looks out through your eyes,
looking at me looking at you, what does it see?
Like you, I was born in the East;
my arms are too long and my spine bowed;
I eat leaves, fruits, and roots; I curl up when I sleep; I live alone.
As your mother once cradled you, mine cradled me,
pushing her nipple between my gums.
Here, where time crawls forward, too slow for human eyes,
neither of us rushes into the future,
since the future means living with a self
that has fed on the squalor that is here.
I cannot tell which of us absorbs the other more;
I am free but you are not,
if freedom means traveling long distances to avoid boredom.
When a child shakes his dirty fist in your face,
making a cry like a buck at rutting time,

you are not impressed. Indolence has made you philosophical.
From where I stand, you are beautiful and ugly, like a weed or
    a human.
We are children meeting for the first time,
each standing in the other's light.
Instruments of darkness have not yet told us truths;
love has not yet made us jealous or cruel,
though it has made us look like one another.
It is understood that part of me lives in you,
or is it the reverse, as it was with my father,
before all of him went into a pint of ash?
Sitting in a miasma of excrement and straw,
combing aside hair matted on your ass,
picking an insect from your breast, chewing a plant bulb,
why are you not appalled by my perfect teeth
and scrupulous dress? How did you lose what God gave you?
Bowing to his unappealable judgment, do you feel a lack?
Nakedness, isolation, bare inanity: these are the soil
and entanglement of actual living.
There are no more elegant redemptive plots.
Roaming about the ape house, I cannot tell which of us,
with naked, painful eyes, is shielded behind Plexiglas.
How can it be that we were not once a family
and now we've come apart? How can it be that it was Adam
who brought death into the world?
Roaming about the ape house, I am sweat and contemplation
    and breath.

I am active and passive, darkness and light, chaste and corrupt.
I am martyr to nothing. I am rejected by nothing.
All the bloated clottings of a life—family disputes, lost inheritances,
vulgar lies, festering love, ungovernable passion, hope wrecked—
bleed out of the mind. Pondering you,
as you chew on a raw onion and ponder me,
I am myself as a boy, showering with my father, learning not to be afraid,
spitting mouthfuls of water into the face of the loved one,
the only thing to suffer for.

Black Camellia

[AFTER PETRARCH]

Little room, with four and a half tatami mats

and sliding paper doors, that used to be

a white, translucent place to live in refined poverty,

what are you now but scalding water in a bath?

Little mattress, that used to fold around me

at sunrise as unfinished dreams were fading,

what are you now but a bloodred palanquin

of plucked feathers and silk airing in the sun?

Weeding the garden, paring a turnip, drinking tea

for want of wine, I flee from my secret love

and from my mind's worm—This is a poem.

Is this a table? No, this is a poem. Am I a girl?—

seeking out the meat-hook crowd I once loathed,

I'm so afraid to find myself alone.

Landscape with Deer and Figure

If you listen, you can hear them chewing

before you see them standing or sitting—

with slim legs and branching antlers—

eating together like children, or the souls

of children, no one animal his own,

as I am my own, watching them watch me,

feeling a fever mount in my forehead,

where all that I am is borne and is effaced

by a herd of deer gathered in the meadow—

like brown ink splashed on rice paper—

abstract, exalted, revealing the eternal harmony,

for only five or six moments, of obligation to family

manifested with such frightful clarity and beauty

it quells the blur of human feeling.

Green Shade

[NARA DEER PARK]

With my head on his spotted back

and his head on the grass—a little bored

with the quiet motion of life

and a cluster of mosquitoes making

hot black dunes in the air—we slept

with the smell of his fur engulfing us.

It was as if my dominant functions were gazing

and dreaming in a field of semiwild deer.

It was as if I could dream what I wanted,

and what I wanted was to long for nothing—

no facts, no reasons—never to say again,

"I want to be like him," and to lie instead

in the hollow deep grass—without esteem or riches—

gazing into the big, lacquer black eyes of a deer.

Myself with Cats

Hanging out the wash, I visit the cats.

"I don't belong to nobody," Yang insists vulgarly.

"Yang," I reply, "you don't know nothing."

Yin, an orange tabby, agrees

but puts kindness ahead of rigid truth.

I admire her but wish she wouldn't idolize

the one who bullies her. I once did that.

Her silence speaks needles when Yang thrusts

his ugly tortoiseshell body against hers,

sprawled in my cosmos. "Really, I don't mind,"

she purrs—her eyes horizontal, her mouth

an Ionian smile, her legs crossed nobly

in front of her, a model of cat Nirvana—

"withholding his affection, he made me stronger."

Pillowcase with Praying Mantis

I found a praying mantis on my pillow.

"What are you praying for?" I asked. "Can you pray

for my father's soul, grasping after Mother?"

Swaying back and forth, mimicking the color

of my sheets, raising her head like a dragon's,

she seemed to view me with deep feeling, as if I were

St. Sebastian bound to a Corinthian column

instead of just Henri lying around reading.

I envied her crisp linearity, as she galloped

slow motion onto my chest, but then she started

mimicking me, lifting her arms in an attitude

of a scholar thinking or romantic suffering.

"Stop!" I sighed, and she did, flying in a wide arc,

like a tiny god-horse hunting for her throne room.

Original Face

Some mornings I wake up kicking like a frog.

My thighs ache from going nowhere all night.

I get up—tailless, smooth skinned, eyes protruding—

and scrub around for my original face.

It is good I am dreaming, I say to myself.

The real characters and events would hurt me.

The real lying, shame, and envy would turn

even a pleasure-loving man into a stone.

Instead, my plain human flesh wakes up

and gazes out at real sparrows skimming the luminous

wet rooftops at the base of a mountain.

No splayed breasts, no glaring teeth appear before me.

Only the ivory hands of morning touching

the real face in the real mirror on my bureau.

Mask

I tied a paper mask onto my face,

my lips almost inside its small red mouth.

Turning my head to the left, to the right,

I looked like someone I once knew, or was,

with straight white teeth and boyish bangs.

My ordinary life had come as far as it would,

like a silver arrow hitting cypress.

Know your place or you'll rue it, I sighed

to the mirror. To succeed, I'd done things

I hated; to be loved, I'd competed promiscuously:

my essence seemed to boil down to only this.

Then I saw my own hazel irises float up,

like eggs clinging to a water plant,

seamless and clear, in an empty, pondlike face.

My Tea Ceremony

Oh, you bowls, don't tell the others I drink

my liquor out of you. I want a feeling of beauty

to surround the plainest facts of my life.

Sitting on my bare heels, making a formal bow,

I want an atmosphere of gentleness to drive

out the squalor of everyday existence

in a little passive house surrounded

by black rocks and gray gravel.

Half cerebral, half sensual, I want to hear

the water murmuring in the kettle

and to see the spider, green as jade,

remaining aloof on the wall.

        Heart, unquiet thing,

I don't want to hate anymore. I want love

to trample through my arms again.

Self-portrait as the Red Princess

When the curtain rises,
        I appear in a red kimono, opening a paper umbrella.
Tucking my elbows into my waist,
        concealing my hands within my sleeves,
I circle the bare stage with tiny steps,
        holding my knees inward,
to create the impression I am small,
        because to be beautiful is to be small,
not young. I end in a dance of tears,
        placing my hand in a simple gesture
in front of my perfect oval face,
        indicating a woman's grief;
I am, after all, a woman,
        and not a man playing a woman.
Even with my mouth painted holly berry red
        and my waxed brows drawn higher,
there is nothing grotesque or cruel
        about my whitened, made-up face.
"The flower of verisimilitude," they call me —
        with my hair done up in a knot
of silver ornaments and lacquered wood
        and with my small melon seed face

filled with carnal love—
               though some nights, sitting for hours
with my numb legs folded under me,
                   pretending I have fallen out of love,
I cannot believe I am refining feminine beauty
                     to a level unsurpassed in life.
Bathing with my lover,
             gazing at his firm stomach covered by hair,
pressing my burning face there,
             and, later, dashing to freedom in the black pines,
I see that I am veering toward destruction,
                 instead of the unity of form and feeling;
I see a dimly shining instrument
                 opening the soft meat of our throats.
Feeding and mating we share with the animals,
                 but volition is ours alone.
Had I not followed a man to death,
                I think I would have died quietly,
as I had lived.

Olympia

Tired, hungry, hot, I climbed the steep slope

to town, a sultry, watery place, crawling with insects

and birds.

      In the semidarkness of the mountain,

small things loomed large: a donkey urinating on a palm;

a salt- and saliva-stained boy riding on his mother's back;

a shy roaming black Adam. I was walking on an edge.

The moments fused into one crystalline rock,

like ice in a champagne bucket. Time was plunging forward,

like dolphins scissoring open water or like me,

following Jenny's flippers down to see the coral reef,

where the color of sand, sea, and sky were merged,

and it was as if that was all God wanted:

not a wife, a house, or a position,

but a self, like a needle, pushing in a vein.

Snow Moon Flower

In this place of rice fields,

metrical mountains, and little bubbling canals,

it was not the self against time

or the self blurred by flesh; it was the self

living without any palpable design.

Common egrets floated on broad bowed wings.

A rooster crowed at dawn and the body—

graceful, alert—slanted gently toward the sun.

In the night gloom, a ground spider jumped

around the shortwave radio

on which a samisen played,

and fawnlike creatures ventured out of the pines,

observing in my windows a solitude

as pure as a bowl of milk.

But outside the gate of this place,

there was another mirror world,

connected only by a dark path of sticky stones,

where there were goat smells and little cries,

hooves pawing and flying beetles. No man could resist it.

No man could endure it. The long shadows

fell on the mind like nails in a plank,

taking one beyond the surface of things,

into the deepest places, not of man's griefs

but of man's truths, which cut deep,

if they did not tear us apart, like a field of thorn,

as the dark tops of the trees shone complacently

and a changing light filtered and breathed

against the lonely surface of everything.

Blur

Little Lamb,
Here I am,
Come and lick
My white neck.

WILLIAM BLAKE

I

It was a Christian idea, sacrificing

oneself to attain the object of one's desire.

I was weak and he was like opium to me,

so present and forceful. I believed I saw myself

through him, as if in a bucket being drawn

up a well, cold and brown as tea.

My horse was wet all that summer.

I pushed him, he pushed me back—proud, lonely,

disappointed—until I rode him,

or he rode me, in tight embrace, and life went on.

I lay whole nights—listless, sighing, gleaming

like a tendril on a tree—withdrawn

into some desiccated realm of beauty.

The hand desired, but the heart refrained.

2

The strong sad ritual between us could not be broken:

the empathetic greeting; the apologies

and reproaches; the narrow bed of his flesh;

the fear of being shown whole in the mirror

of another's fragmentation; the climbing on;

the unambiguous freedom born of submission;

the head, like a rock, hefted on and off moist earth;

the rough language; the impermeable core

of one's being made permeable; the black hair

and shining eyes; and afterward, the marrowy

emissions, the gasping made liquid; the torso,

like pale clay or a plank, being dropped;

the small confessional remarks that inscribe

the soul; the indolence; the being alone.

3

Then everything decanted and modulated,

as it did in a horse's eye, and the self—

pure, classical, like a figure carved from stone—

was something broken off again.

Two ways of being: one, seamless

saturated color (not a bead of sweat),

pure virtuosity, bolts of it; the other,

raw and unsocialized, "an opera of impurity,"

like super-real sunlight on a bruise.

I didn't want to have to choose.

It didn't matter anymore what was true

and what was not. Experience was not facts,

but uncertainty. Experience was not events,

but feelings, which I would overcome.

4

Waking hungry for flesh, stalking flesh

no matter where—in the dunes, at the Pantheon,

in the Tuileries, at the White Party—

cursing and fumbling with flesh, smelling flesh,

clutching flesh, sucking violently on flesh,

cleaning up flesh, smiling at flesh, running away

from flesh, and later loathing flesh,

half of me was shattered, half was not,

like a mosaic shaken down by earthquake.

All the things I loved—a horse, a wristwatch,

a hall mirror—and all the things I endeavored to be—

truthful, empathetic, funny—presupposed

a sense of self locked up in a sphere,

which would never be known to anyone.

5

Running, lifting, skipping rope at the gym,

I was a man like a bronze man;

I was my body—with white stones

in my eye sockets, soldered veins in my wrists,

and a delicately striated, crepelike scrotum.

Sighs, grunts, exhales, salt stains, dingy mats,

smeared mirrors, and a faintly sour smell

filled the gulf between the mind and the world,

but the myth of love for another remained

bright and plausible, like an athlete painted

on the slope of a vase tying his sandal.

In the showers, tears fell from our hair,

as if from bent glistening sycamores.

It was as if earth were taking us back.

6

In front of me, you are sleeping. I sleep also.

Probably you are right that I project

the ambiguities of my own desires.

I feel I only know you at the edges.

Sometimes in the night I jump up panting,

see my young gray head in the mirror,

and fall back, as humans do, from the cold glass.

I don't have the time to invest in what

I purport to desire. But when you open

your eyes shyly and push me on the shoulder,

all I am is impulse and longing

pulled forward by the rope of your arm,

I, flesh-to-flesh, sating myself

on blurred odors of the soft black earth.

Blackbird and Wolf

2007

Sycamores

I came from a place with a hole in it,

my body once its body, behind a beard of hair.

And after I emerged, all dripping wet,

heavy drops came out of my eyes, touching its face.

I kissed its mouth; I bit it with my gums.

I lay on it like a snail on a cup,

my body, whatever its nature was,

revealed to me by its body. I did not know

I was powerless before a strange force.

I did not know life cheats us. All I knew,

nestling my head in its soft throat pouch,

was a hard, gemlike feeling burning through me,

like limbs of burning sycamores, touching

across some new barrier of touchability.

Mimosa Sensitiva

Polishing your eyeglasses, I try them on

and watch the nurses hoist you—blind, giggling,

muttering nonsense French. For a moment, like a spider,

you dangle at the edge of the present,

pondering who I am: "Ma, I'm Henri.

You made me." Then my eyes flee the here-and-now.

You're pulling yourself out of the deep end,

your skin like the seamless emulsion on a strip of film.

Sensuality is confirming beauty. I'm eleven again.

Then the banal shatters everything.

In a tangled nightgown, your skin marsupial,

you're pawing through leaf mulch for pain medicine

you can't function without. The thrash of your hands

smolders like wet black ash.

In Chinese, the basic phonetic value of horse, *ma*,

turns up in the word for mother.

"Horse-mother, look!" I cry. Soldier-ants

are suckling on the big pink heads of your peonies.

Horse-mother flickers like a candle in the dark.

Horse-mother, why does your mouth have a grim set?

I know that all beneath the sky decays.

I know that you once cradled me in sleep,

your belly empty as a purse. "Horse-mother, look!"

I repeat. The mimosa tree is going to sleep,

its tiny pinnate leaves closing and drooping,

like you, sensitive to light and touch,

mimicking death when I push a needle into you

and bright beads run out, as from a draining bird.

Gulls

Naked, hairy, trembling, I dove into the green,

where I saw a bulky form that was Mother

in her pink swimsuit, pushing out of water,

so I kicked deeper, beyond a sugar boat

and Blake's Ulro and Beulah; beyond grief, fate;

fingers, toes, and skin; beyond speech,

plagues of the blood, and flowers thrown on a coffin;

beyond eros and the disease of incompleteness;

and as I swam, I saw myself against the sky

and against the light, a tiny human knot with eyes,

my numb hands and repeated motion, like the gulls aloft,

touching the transparent structure of the world,

and in that icy, green, silvery frothing,

I was straightening all that I had made crooked.

Oil & Steel

My father lived in a dirty-dish mausoleum,

watching a portable black-and-white television,

reading the *Encyclopaedia Britannica,*

which he preferred to Modern Fiction.

One by one, his schnauzers died of liver disease,

except the one that guarded his corpse

found holding a tumbler of Bushmills.

"Dead is dead," he would say, an antipreacher.

I took a plaid shirt from the bedroom closet

and some motor oil — my inheritance.

Once I saw him weep in a courtroom —

neglected, needing nursing — this man who never showed

me much affection but gave me a knack

for solitude, which has been mostly useful.

Twilight

There's a black bear
in the apple tree
and he won't come down.
I can hear him panting,
like an athlete.
I can smell the stink
of his body.

Come down, black bear.
Can you hear me?

The mind is the most interesting thing to me;
like the sudden death of the sun,
it seems implausible that darkness will swallow it
or that anything is lost forever there,
like a black bear in a fruit tree,
gulping up sour apples
with dry sucking sounds,

or like us at the pier, somber and tired,
making food from sunlight,
you saying a word, me saying a word, trying hard,

though things were disintegrating.
Still, I wanted you,
your lips on my neck,
your postmodern sexuality.
Forlorn and anonymous:
I didn't want to be that. I could hear
the great barking monsters of the lower waters
calling me forward.

You see, my mind takes me far,
but my heart dreams of return.
Black bear,
with pale-pink tongue
at the center of his face,
is turning his head,
like the face of Christ from life.
Shaking the apple boughs,
he is stronger than I am
and seems so free of passion—
no fear, no pain, no tenderness. I want to be that.

Come down, black bear,
I want to learn the faith of the indifferent.

To Sleep

Then out of the darkness leapt a bare hand

that stroked my brow: "Come along, child;

stretch out your feet under the blanket.

Darkness will give you back, unremembering.

Do not be afraid." So I put down my book

and pushed like a finger through sheer silk,

the autobiographical part of me, the *am*,

snatched up to a different place, where I was

no longer my body but something more—

the compulsive, disorderly parts of me

in a state of equalization, everything sliding off:

war, suicide, love, poverty—as the rebellious,

mortal I, I, I lay, like a beetle irrigating a rose,

my red thoughts in a red shade all I was.

The Tree Cutters

You can't see them and then you can,

like bear cubs in the treetops working for man,

hoisting one another with ropes and pulleys

that seem the clearest possible metaphor

for bright feelings vs. dark feelings,

as I lie in the grass below, hearing the big limbs fall,

like lightning exploding on the lake.

Once, a thick, dirty, bad-smelling sorrow

covered me like old meat: I saw a bloodstained toad,

instead of my white kitten; I saw shadows and misprision,

instead of my milk and pancakes. "Maybe God has gone away,"

my life moaned, hugging my knees, my teeth, my terrible pride,

though after a time, like a warm chrysalis, it produced

a tough, lustrous thread the pale yellow of onions.

Self-portrait with Hornets

Hornets, two hornets, buzz over my head;

I'm napping and cannot keep my eyes open.

"Do you come from far away?" I ask, dozing off.

My gums are dry when I wake. A morning breeze

rakes the treetops. I can smell the earth.

The two hornets are puzzling over

something sticky on my night table,

wiping their gold heads with their arms.

Ordinary things are like symbols. My eyes are watery

and blurred. Then I lose myself again.

I'm walking slowly in a heat haze,

my vision contracting to a tiny porthole,

drawing me to it, like flourishing palms.

I can feel blood draining out of my face.

I can feel my heart beating inside my heart,

the self receding from the center of the picture.

I can taste sugar under my tongue.

All the usual human plots of ascent

and triumph appear disrupted.

Crossing my ankles, I watch the day

vibrate around me, watch the geraniums

climb toward the distant mountains

where I was born, watch the black worm

wiggling out of the window box,

hiding its head from the pale sun

that lies down on everything,

purifying it. Lord, teach me to live.

Teach me to love. Lie down on me.

Gravity and Center

I'm sorry I cannot say I love you when you say

you love me. The words, like moist fingers,

appear before me full of promise but then run away

to a narrow black room that is always dark,

where they are silent, elegant, like antique gold,

devouring the thing I feel. I want the force

of attraction to crush the force of repulsion

and my inner and outer worlds to pierce

one another, like a horse whipped by a man.

I don't want words to sever me from reality.

I don't want to need them. I want nothing

to reveal feeling but feeling—as in freedom,

or the knowledge of peace in a realm beyond,

or the sound of water poured in a bowl.

American Kestrel

I see you sitting erect on my fire escape,

plucking at your dinner of flayed mouse,

like the red strings of a harp, choking a bit

on the venous blue flesh and hemorrhaging tail.

With your perfect black-and-white thief's mask,

you look like a stuffed bird in a glass case,

somewhere between the animal and human life.

The love word is far away. Can you see me?

I am a man. No one has what I have:

my long clean hands, my bored lips. This is my home:

Woof-woof, the dog utters, afraid of emptiness,

as I am, so my soul attaches itself to things,

trying to create something neither confessional

nor abstract, like the moon breaking through the pines.

Homosexuality

First I saw the round bill, like a bud;

then the sooty crested head, with avernal eyes

flickering, distressed, then the peculiar

long neck wrapping and unwrapping itself,

like pity or love, when I removed the stovepipe

cover of the bedroom chimney to free

what was there and a duck crashed into the room

(I am here in this fallen state), hitting her face,

bending her throat back (my love, my inborn

turbid wanting, at large all night), backing away,

gnawing at her own wing linings (the poison of my life,

the beast, the wolf), leaping out the window,

which I held open (now clear, sane, serene),

before climbing back naked into bed with you.

Poppies

Waking from comalike sleep, I saw the poppies,

with their limp necks and unregimented beauty.

Pause, I thought, say something true: it was night,

I wanted to kiss your lips, which remained supple,

but all the water in them had been replaced

with embalming compound. So I was angry.

I loved the poppies, with their wide-open faces,

how they carried themselves, beckoning to me

instead of pushing away. The way in and the way out

are the same, essentially: emotions disrupting thought,

proximity to God, the pain of separation.

I loved the poppies, with their effortless existence,

like grief and fate, but tempered and formalized.

Your hair was black and curly; I combed it.

Bowl of Lilacs

My lilacs died today, floating in a bowl.

All week I watched them pushing away,

their pruned heads swollen together into something

like anger, making a brief comeback

toward the end, as if secretly embalmed.

Just before your death, I cut your hair,

so when you were laid out, you looked like yourself.

Then some men screwed planks over your coffin.

I held a towel to my face. Once, in a light-bathed kitchen,

naked and blissfully myself, I scrambled us eggs

and felt the act of looking and perceiving

was no longer something understood

from the exterior. It was pure being:

saturated and raw as a bowl of lilacs.

Shaving

Outstretched in the tub, like a man in a tomb,

I pull the razor across my face and throat.

The bathroom is pristine, spare, without any clear

conflict; I like that. The cells in my skin

draw heat to themselves, like grape bunches.

In the silver hand mirror, my youthful

shyness is gone now. I lie bent, turned in,

but supple, pliant. I was rough on you;

I know this because you told me, but you

held up well. Trees, mammals, fire, snow—

they are like emotions. Through our eyes,

pain comes in (my doctor told me this),

but how does it exit, if you're looking forward

and I'm looking back, my big, unlovely head

(you called it that) feverish, then shivery?

My Weed

On the path to the water, I found an ugly weed

growing between rocks. The wind was stroking it,

saying, "My weed, my weed." Its solid,

hairy body rose up, with big silver leaves

that rubbed off on me, like sex. At first,

I thought it was a lamb's ear, but it wasn't.

I'm not a member of the ugly school,

but I circled around it and looked a lot,

which is to say, I was just being, and it seemed to me—

in a higher sense—to represent the sanity of living.

It was twilight. Planets were gathering.

"Mr. Weed," I said, "I'm competitive,

I'm afraid, I'm isolated, I'm bright.

Can you tell me how to survive?"

Self-portrait with Red Eyes

Throughout our affair of eleven years,

disappearing into the pleasure-unto-death

acts I recall now as love and, afterward,

orbiting through the long, deep sleeps

in which memory, motor of everything,

reconstituted itself, I cared nothing about

life outside the walls of our bedroom.

The hand erasing writes the real thing,

and I am trying. I loved life and see now

this was a weakness. I loved the little

births and deaths occurring in us daily.

Even the white spit on your sharp teeth

was the foam of love, saying to me: It is not true,

after all, that you were never loved.

Beach Walk

I found a baby shark on the beach.

Seagulls had eaten his eyes. His throat was bleeding.

Lying on shell and sand, he looked smaller than he was.

The ocean had scraped his insides clean.

When I poked his stomach, darkness rose up in him,

like black water. Later, I saw a boy,

aroused and elated, beckoning from a dune.

Like me, he was alone. Something tumbled between us—

not quite emotion. I could see the pink

interior flesh of his eyes. "I got lost. Where am I?"

he asked, like a debt owed to death.

I was pressing my face to its spear hafts.

We fall, we fell, we are falling. Nothing mitigates it.

The dark embryo bares its teeth and we move on.

Dead Wren

When I open your little gothic wings

on my whitewashed chest of drawers,

I almost fear you, as if today were my funeral.

Moment by moment, enzymes digest

your life into a kind of coffin liqueur.

Two flies, like coroners, investigate your feathers.

My clock is your obelisk, though only this morning

you lunged into my room, extravagant as Nero,

then, not seeing yourself in the sunlit glass,

struck it. Night—what beams does it clear away?

The rain falls. The sky is pained. All that breathes suffers.

Yet the waters of affliction are purifying.

The wounded soldier heals. There is new wine and oil.

Here, take my handkerchief as your hearse.

To the Forty-third President

Hip deep in the pit, wading through ruins

of that border state where the mind narrows

and will not be broadened by hope,

I hear your strong victorious voice

and almost believe love of country

will be enough to right old wrongs,

pity the poor, and avert war,

but then the soft-pedaling language resumes,

you lick your lips nervously,

veering toward arrogance,

and my head aches all over again.

What I see are tactical endurance,

rhetoric divorced from practice, and aversion

squatting on a shaky platform.

When you place your hand on the Bible,

do you think about eternal questions:

Why are we here instead of nothing?

Does love make us who we are?

Do we survive death? Like Jesus,

my father's people were sprinkled on their foreheads;

they farmed peaches and tobacco.

My mother's people fled invading armies

of Romans, Persians, and Turks.

Can a few like you lead us all?

Waving from your droning black helicopter

at the cheering hordes, fixing your gaze

on some mythical past, can you see

time battering the surface of Earth?

Can you see sorrow is egalitarian?

Or the hairy leg of Satan planted firmly

in poverty, where the birth of suffering

supersedes the birth of perfect children?

Nature seems complacent

as hate rains down on us in swoops.

Why does God make man feel it?

Part of me, the real red-bloodedness,

open, drinking in the night, hates something vaguely, too,

and is frightened, staring out at the night grass

where, when the moon breaks out for a minute,

steam rises from ropes of excrement

extruded by some unbroken animal

circling in the dark wood.

Dune

I have a fever which I'm treating with gin.

A war is lingering, but I feel distanced from it.

I think I'm at the lowest level of actual control,

lying around in black swimming trunks,

staring out at treetops and cobalt blue,

an innocent combination pouring hunger

through my heart. A pink butterfly capers

over the cosmos, where it got lost this morning.

Is it straight from God, the freedom?

I want to write something highly controlled

that is the opposite, like a dizzy

honeycomb gleaming with amber light.

I love the light of the water shellacking

my arms and legs, like something from Ovid.

Each day begins with lavender light

moving through my room, like an open hand,

and the call of birds out my window

and butter-and-eggs and adult bees searching

for the sweet, white, four-petaled violets

and hunchbacked loons in flight, projecting

their feet out behind, like me in my twin bed,

pressing my face into nothing, until afternoon

arrives, and I swim across the bay under

a white sun, its arms beckoning over

endless blue, my back and shoulders darkening,

like the raked earth. I feel protection

under the law, if the law is light. In the woods,

afterward, I pick blueberries.

While I am writing this, the cat scratches herself

and rubs her belly against my knees, purring.

She'll stretch out soon on my books and bills.

On the horizon, a sailboat is going nowhere:

"Remain awhile, drink a cocktail," it pleads,

and I do. How sad my footprints look

in the dunes, like a single voice

raised in lament, looking for liberation.

A white cloud overhead moves too quickly,

casting shadows, and all the people of the shore say,

"Oh, how lovely," but I don't believe it is at all.

I think of something being extinguished.

Sometimes, I feel like a large, open eye,

in which there is a sifting of too many things:

a summer fever, brushstrokes of green larches,

yellow ray flowers, Japanese beetles copulating

everywhere, war, and a cut-glass tumbler of gin—

all these scraps, like some eternal revenue

of memory and feeling blown together.

My lips nibble out of control,

like creatures differentiating themselves,

trying to give inwardness voice. "Oh,

let him be," God is saying, "I made him."

Down on the lawn, a campfire snaps violently

as the coals are stirred with a poker,

burning the beetles in frenzied masses.

Still, the earth forms, stems flourish,

and the time of my life goes on.

Yesterday, a storm tore the bay apart.

I was swimming and became disoriented.

Violent scrolls of foam and green water

rolled across the silky, pellucid surface

and lightning stained everything red

as I stroked through showers of arrows.

The little tree of knowledge with my name on it

wasn't anywhere for me to climb onto.

Throw a man into the sea and he becomes a fish,

but still, the sound was unsettling—

its foaming energy, its vibrant mutability.

Then I lay facedown in wet sand,

my arms strung with strands of seaweed,

as I rolled over, trembling,

and a solid blackbird flew into view,

catching a bee in its mouth, calling to mind

the purple wild thyme that grows on lawns

in these northern parts, tawny bees murmuring

over them on their way home to sleep and safety,

remaking them when nature beats them apart,

putting their whole lives into the small sting

that hurts us, but not before changing gum

into gold, like poetry, which is stronger

than I am and makes me do what it wants.

Is there something in earth that makes us resemble them—

rising at dawn, the sun flashing scarlet,

rubbing together for warmth, going forward—

even when the world seems just a heap of broken things?

ACKNOWLEDGMENTS

For their encouragement, I am indebted to the editors
of the following publications, where poems, sometimes
in different form, were originally published.

"Ape House, Berlin Zoo": *The American Poetry Review*
"Mimosa Sensitiva": *The American Poetry Review*
"Self-portrait with Hornets": *The American Poetry Review*
"Ascension on Fire Island": *Antaeus*
"V-winged and Hoary": *Antaeus*
"The Annulment": *The Atlantic Monthly*
"Black Camellia": *The Atlantic Monthly*
"Dead Wren": *The Atlantic Monthly*
"Horses": *The Atlantic Monthly*
"Landscape with Deer and Figure": *The Atlantic Monthly*
"Tarantula": *Columbia: A Magazine of Poetry and Prose*
"The Zoo Wheel of Knowledge": *The Gettysburg Review*
"The Marble Queen": *The Nation*
"The Mare": *The Nation*
"Icarus Breathing": *The New Republic*
"Mask": *The New Republic*
"My Tea Ceremony": *The New Republic*
"The Pink and the Black": *The New Republic*
"American Kestrel": *The New Yorker*
"Bowl of Lilacs": *The New Yorker*
"Chiffon Morning": *The New Yorker*

"40 Days and 40 Nights": *The New Yorker*
"Gravity and Center": *The New Yorker*
"Gulls": *The New Yorker*
"Homosexuality": *The New Yorker*
"Myself with Cats": *The New Yorker*
"Paper Dolls": *The New Yorker*
"Pillowcase with Praying Mantis": *The New Yorker*
"Poppies": *The New Yorker*
"Radiant Ivory": *The New Yorker*
"Self-portrait in a Gold Kimono": *The New Yorker*
"Self-portrait with Red Eyes": *The New Yorker*
"Snow Moon Flower": *The New Yorker*
"To the Forty-third President": *The New Yorker*
"The Tree Cutters": *The New Yorker*
"Twilight": *The New Yorker*
"White Spine": *The New Yorker*
"You Come When I Call You": *The New Yorker*
"Apollo": *The Paris Review*
"Sycamores": *The Paris Review*
"*Une Lettre à New York*": *The Paris Review*
"To Sleep": *Ploughshares*
"Father's Jewelry Box": *Poetry*
"A Half-life": *Poetry*
"The Roman Baths at Nîmes": *Provincetown Arts*
"Beach Walk": *Salmagundi*
"Toxicology": *Salmagundi*
"Oil & Steel": *The Threepenny Review*
"Apostasy": *The Yale Review*
"The Hare": *The Yale Review*
"The Minimum Circus": *The Yale Review*
"Shaving": *The Yale Review*

9 780374 532666